# The Trouble with Mr. Adams

Gord Rand

*The Trouble with Mr. Adams*
first published 2017 by
Scirocco Drama
An imprint of J. Gordon Shillingford Publishing Inc.
© 2017, Gord Rand

Scirocco Drama Editor: Glenda MacFarlane
Cover design by Terry Gallagher/Doowah Design Inc.
Author photo by Angela Besharah
Production photos by Cylla von Tiedemann
Printed and bound in Canada on 100% post-consumer recycled paper.

We acknowledge the financial support of the Manitoba Arts Council and
The Canada Council for the Arts for our publishing program.

For production inquiries, please contact:
Ian Arnold, Catalyst Entertainment
#312 – 100 Broadview Ave.
Toronto, ON
Canada
M4M 3H3
416-645-0935
ian@catalysttcm.com

www.catalysttcm.com

Library and Archives Canada Cataloguing in Publication

Rand, Gord, author
    The trouble with Mr. Adams / Gord Rand.

A play.
ISBN 978-1-927922-35-4 (softcover)

    I. Title.

PS8635.A524T76 2017      C812'.6      C2017-904840-6

J. Gordon Shillingford Publishing
P.O. Box 86, RPO Corydon Avenue, Winnipeg, MB Canada R3M 3S3

*To my beautiful wife, Jeanie Calleja. You are my rock.*

# Foreword

Before reading *The Trouble with Mr. Adams*, I already knew that Gord Rand was a provocateur. And I mean that in the best creative sense. First of all, Gord is a great actor. I was lucky enough to get the chance to direct him in *The Philanderer* at the Shaw Festival in the summer of 2014. He played the philanderer of the title (a charming flamethrower) and was extremely good at it because he knew that provoking an audience — and even his fellow actors — is the best way to make something exciting happen onstage. And that's really our job in the theatre: to shake up conventional ideas, to make something surprising happen right before the audience's eyes. To say the unsayable, to upset the status quo; that's what it's all about. And to have fun while doing it. Gord's funny, bracing, charming but alarming choices are a perfect match for Shaw, who was the most wonderfully bristling writer himself. Shaw's plays are invitations to an argument. And so is Gord Rand's *The Trouble with Mr. Adams*.

The trouble referred to in the title of this play is caused by a dangerous relationship between a high school girls' volleyball coach, Gary Adams, and his star player. Mr. Adams begins the play in the haze of complete love and obsession; he believes that he has kept himself on the right side of the fine line between thought and illegal action. On the surface, this is a play that asks us to empathize with a man who may be a pedophile. And it's not a responsible, moral tale where that man is wrongfully accused, or where he finally confesses and repents. This is a story where the man is unabashed in his passion for Mercedes, his star player. Right away, in the first scene, he acknowledges to his stunned, acerbic wife that he is obsessed with this girl. Yes, he claims he hasn't actually done anything wrong, but isn't lust for this young woman a crime in and of itself? And what was he thinking, spending time alone with her at their latest out-of-town game?

These moral questions provide the motor for this unusual play, but it's the bracing humour and the brisk, dynamic language that make the play sing. The dialogue sizzles and pops, and makes hairpin turns. There is a kind of rollicking, absurdist poetry to the things these characters say to each other—even just looking at the page, you can feel that energy. It's as if the absurdity of Ionesco's *The Bald Soprano* was translated into the lives of a small-town Canadian coach and the three women he spars with.

And then there is the element of surprise. That's what really hooked me. You just never know what these four characters might say next. The play is structured in three long one-on-one matches, or volleys. Watching the arguments, the navigations, the proposals and counter-proposals fly is kind of like watching a thrilling sporting event. Ping-pong. Tennis. Sometimes chess. These characters are bobbing and weaving, spiking the ball, speaking even before they think. These characters are looking for a weak spot. They are flying across the court to return a demonic serve.

Those three duets are technically challenging, which we learned when we got to put the premiere production together at the bold Tarragon Theatre in the fall of 2015. In the Tarragon production, set designer Kimberly Purtell and I decided to magnify the sporting energy of the play by seating the audience in two banks, facing each other, stadium-style. This meant the audience could see audience, the actors could see everybody, and everyone was a part of the live action in the room. There were gasps, as we expected, but also there were laughs and nods and the kind of forward-leaning intensity that we all aim for in the theatre. And the play provoked conversation afterwards, as we knew it would.

Each of the scenes in *Mr. Adams* is a wonderfully layered, dense interaction. Since Gord is an actor, he writes material that gives actors room to create, but also demands a kind of bravery. Each one of the four characters in this play makes choices that could be unpopular, says things that could—and should—produce gasps in the audience. The play's real subject is the difficulties of growing older, both for men and for women. The minefield of passion, and the cost of acting on that passion: each of the characters in *The Trouble with Mr. Adams* navigates this dangerous game with wit and surprising candour.

In the first long scene, Gary Adams and his wife struggle to understand where their marriage stands. Peggy—Gary's wife—is blistering in her attacks on her wayward husband, and the heat of those attacks is refreshing and shocking to them both. It's clear that this was a wonderful marriage, and that the loss of it will devastate them. Peggy's wicked sense of humour, and Gary's surprising desire to speak the truth keep the scene spinning into the unexpected. In the second scene, Gary goes head-to-head with Barbara Middleton, a lawyer for the teacher's union who is ostensibly preparing his defence, but in building it she attacks Mr. Adams's certainty about having done nothing wrong. It is a vigorous cat-and-mouse game, and by the end of it we can feel the scope of the trouble that Mr. Adams has made for himself, and for his family. The third and final scene is a surprise reunion between Gary and the object of his desire, Mercedes. It is a dangerous scene, and one in which the young woman is not a victim; we can finally understand the complicated currents in the relationship that fuelled the devastating mistakes that Mr. Adams made. By the end, we find ourselves empathizing in surprising directions. The trouble that Mr. Adams has created is complex, and wicked, and human.

I'm very proud to have been a part of the first production of this radical play. We need writers in the theatre who aren't afraid to flip our assumptions on their heads. And who have fun doing it.


Lisa Peterson
May 2017

# Gord Rand

Gord Rand is an actor and a writer. He has been on stages from San Francisco to Kigali. Favourite roles include *Hamlet*, *Oedipus Rex*, and *The Philanderer*. He's been on TV and in the movies too: *Maps to the Stars*, *Orphan Black*, *Cardinal*, *Taken*, and *Pure*.

Gord has written five plays: *Dogs*, *Orgy in the Lighthouse*, *Pond Life*, *The Trial of Thumbelina*, and *The Trouble with Mr. Adams*. He is currently working on his sixth. He recently completed a film based on his play *Pond Life*, as well as a feature documentary called *Goodness in Rwanda*.

Gord is lucky: he has two lovely kids, a beautiful wife, and a large, slobbery dog. They love to snuggle in the winter to stay warm.

# Acknowledgements

Many thanks to:

Andrea Donaldson, Andrea Romaldi, and Richard Rose at Tarragon for their unwavering support, questions, and suggestions.

All my pals who read and listened for wine: Jeanie Calleja, Kristian Bruun, Julian Richings, Jenny Young, Fiona Highet, MJ Shaw, Chris Howden, Susanna Fournier, Kerry McPherson, Ben Campbell, and Peter Hutt.

For early conversations with the late, great Gina Wilkinson.

For all the Playwright Unit's feedback — Marie Beath Badian, Amy Lee Lavoie, Jordi Mand, Marilo Nunez, and Adam Paolozza.

And a special thanks to my family: Jeanie, JJ, Hughie, Peter, Cynthia, Tom, Marc, all the cousins and all the in-laws for their constant support in an unsteady industry. But especially Lisa Peterson, who honoured me with her wit, sparkle, hilarity, rigour, intelligence, and grace.

# Playwright's notes

I think a protagonist—or any dramatic character—need not be likeable to be compelling. *The Trouble with Mr. Adams* is a monster story and the theatre, to me, is one of the last safe arenas to publicly engage in scary role-play and daring exploration. Like my friend Ross Manson says, theatre is "a candle we use to peer safely into the darkness." I hope *The Trouble with Mr. Adams* disturbs and provokes.

There has been some debate about the law in the play. Where I'm from, it is a legal offence for a figure in a position of power to abuse that power with respect to any ward under eighteen. However, in the practice of prosecution, emphasis differs. In most legal cases, there are gradations of punishment—some judicial and others social. Barbara focuses on the younger, more common age of consent, sixteen, as it increases the likelihood of damaging legal and personal repercussions for Gary. I think a sixteen-year-old alleged victim elicits an almost universal, less-rational reaction from the public than an eighteen-year-old alleged victim. It corners him into making the awful choice he makes.

A word about the sex scene in Act One: Anybody interested in producing the play is welcome to have a conversation with me about it. It's daring; it plays an interesting game with an audience's relationship with sex, and it requires nudity. So much to recommend it! But still...it may be a good cut. In all seriousness, the scene led to illuminating and productive discussion, so we decided to keep it in the original production. But if it is a sticking point for any potential producers, the play can be effective without it, and I'm happy to discuss cutting it.

The script is a jumping-off point for actors to get into each other's heads and hearts and mess around. I like it when lines are said over top of each other; I like it when characters try to interrupt each other, and I even like it when they test their improvising skills. So I don't like writing down '/' for when one actor is supposed to cut another actor off. There are some sections that are written in dual dialogue with suggestions for when lines intercut—but if both characters are gunning as hard for the win, they won't always listen and they sometimes shout and the acting can change with the day. For example, there's a bit where Gary has to do some "coaching." The actor can freshly improvise this each night, or improvise during rehearsal for something set for the performance, or a mixture of both. My main advice is to get good actors and let them pursue their goals with extreme prejudice.

# Production history

*The Trouble with Mr. Adams* premiered at the Tarragon Theatre on October 20, 2015, with the following cast and creative team:

Gary Adams ........................................ Chris Earle

Peggy Adams ........................ Philippa Domville

Barbara Middleton ...................... Allegra Fulton

Mercedes McPfefferidge .......... Sydney Owchar


Directed by Lisa Peterson
Stage Manager — Sandy Plunkett
Sound Design — Todd Charlton
Costume Design — Charlotte Dean
Lighting and Set Design — Kim Purtell
Fight Director — John Stead
Script Coordinator — Leah Holder

Chris Earle and Philippa Domville in *The Trouble with Mr. Adams*.

Allegra Fulton in *The Trouble with Mr. Adams*.

Sydney Owchar and Chris Earle in *The Trouble with Mr. Adams.*

Chris Earle in *The Trouble with Mr. Adams*.

# Characters

Gary Adams
45, high school volleyball coach
and teacher.

Peggy Adams
45, high school English teacher
and Gary's wife.

Barbara Middleton
45, lawyer sent from
the teacher's union.

Mercedes McPfefferidge
18, star volleyball player
on Gary's team.

# A note on formatting

The dialogue is written in columns, each corresponding with
one of the characters' lines. It's a little unusual, but I think
it helps with the rhythm of reading it and the volley-and-
response nature of the dialogue.

# ACT ONE

*GARY has just arrived home. He stands in front of his wife PEGGY, holding an Adidas gym bag, wearing a cheap team windbreaker — in school colours — with matching slacks. Around his neck is a medal from the OFSAA Jr Girls Volleyball tournament. PEGGY sits across from him, wearing a bathrobe.*

PEGGY:

GARY:

I'm leaving you.

It'll be great.

It'll be better.

I'll stay at Mike's until I can find my own place.
He's in Disneyland with his girlfriend.
She hates it.
Which is weird.
But he's lovin' it!
So they'll be there until the end of the week.
And then they're driving back, so…

Lots of time to clean the sheets.

*Pause.*

You had a couple good days
away then, eh?

*GARY smiles.*

Not bad, yeah.

And here I thought you were
trying to get home in time
for our sex date.

Our what?

The day we have sex. The
day you fold yourself into
me and we stare into the
middle distance waiting for
affirmation of our physical
love.

That's today?

Tomorrow, actually. Tuesday.
Tomorrow and tomorrow
and tomorrow.
Today's Monday. Still.
What did you do with the
weekend, Gary?
Dazzled by circumstance?

OFSAA. Girls' volleyball
championship.
You knew that.

I did.

We won.

Wow.

Champs. Three years in a
row now.

Magic.

You could say that, yeah.

So what days would you
want the kids?

Week on, week off?
That sound doable?

How about me? You wanna
ask me about my day?

Should we have a glass of
wine, or beer or something?

Because that's how this is
done?

Really?
Ok.
How was your day?

That was a bit flat, Gary.
Throw a few notes in there, a
minor scale maybe.
Make it sound natural.

I don't know what that
means.

You're not a hero, Gary.
You're just a guy leaving his
wife a few weeks after her
forty-fifth birthday.
So let's try it again.
With more feeling.
Modulate your voice a little.
Just so I can pretend to
believe it.
It's probably the last time
you'll ask me, so let's pay
some fucking attention here,
don'tcha think?

How was your day?

*PEGGY looks at him. A parody of dissatisfaction.*

A kid barfed on me today.

Oh, wow.

At the food court.

Gross.

Orange Julius.

Sounds like a story.

Not really.

OK.

It wasn't a cute baby or
anything.

It wasn't spit-up.

Remember innocence? All
the stuff that came out of
Jessica and Jaime? It was like
Elvish fluid. Even their pee
seemed magical.

Chardonnay is white, right?

But this wasn't a baby. This
was an adolescent boy.
An adolescent boy who
should have known better.
Staring at me with his mouth
open.

Feeling so much with no
way to say it.

A boy becomes a man.

Ugh.

You can have the house.

I have no idea how to
express the existential
slugging I took at that
moment.

*PEGGY begins commenting as though*
*watching a movie of herself.*

As my camera pulled up,
and I saw all of the Greater
Whitby Area, with me at the
centre of it.
In my useful pants.

Alone at a table outside
Laura Secord's.

They still have those?

Three.

Stop checking your fucking
phone.

With Orange Julius splashed
all over my functional shoes.

Pooling in the creases of my
thighs.

And you… Somewhere else.

>It's gonna be better.
>For both of us.

*Pause.*

But! I shook it off.
Not literally. That stuff
soaks in.
Emotionally.
Chicks are great like that.
We just… get on with
our day.
So I did. I got on with
my day.
I drove Jessica to violin.
That was at 3:15. And at 4:00
I dropped Jaime off at ballet.
And nobody said anything.

>*Wishing she were still young enough to find it weird.*

Isn't that weird?!
I did my whole day with that
boy's upchuck on me.
And nobody said anything.
Not at Foodland, not at Tot
Tailor's, not at Magicuts.
Nobody.

>Welcome to middle age.

Thank you. Right?
Kind of like your weekend.

I guess they just thought it
was normal.
I guess they just thought
that's what mums are for.
Vomit depositories.

               What's that?

A place you leave something
you don't want anymore.

               Suppository?

No, that's something you
shove up your ass.

               That's not what mums are
               for.

Just wives?

*Pause.*

               Should we have that
               glass of wine, or a beer or
               something?

Because that's how this is
done?

               That's how it could be done.

Because we're adults?

               I don't hate you, Peg.

Because we're grown-ups?

               The opposite.

What exactly is the opposite
of hate?

               You wanted him to flirt with
               you.

I what?

               Sexy, middle-aged woman
               like yourself.
               That's what usually happens,
               isn't it?

Is it?

               And you flirt back.
               And la-di-da.

Jesus, Gary.
You used to be happy. You
used to whistle through this
house like a bird.
You used to flit through this
house with your wrench and
your screwdriver, fixing this
and fixing that.
Like you were in love, Gary.

                                    What can I say?

I used to pause on the phone
with my mother so she could
hear you whistling in the
background.

                                    What can I say?

Whistling through the house
you owned with me.

                                    What can I tell you?

You can tell me what you
should have told me seven
months ago.
When a man cries alone in
his trophy room his wife
tends to worry.

                                    Peg.
You need to know: I never
cheated on you.

Gary, don't do it so I hate
you.

                                    I had serious rules. 1. Be kind
to my wife. This is not her
fault. Listen to what she is
saying.
Even if you have to mouth
the words as she's saying
them so you can stay on
track, do that. Because she's
your wife, and she deserves
for you to try.

My Sorrento.

Oh wow.

Number 2. Don't make an idiot out of yourself. Don't drive your Sorrento—
—over there at 3:00 in the morning, and park outside her house waiting for her bathroom light to come on so you can imagine her in the shower.

And number 3: Fuck. Not. Her. Seriously.

It's not right, it's not right, it's not right.

Even though I could feel my balls and cock basically detaching themselves from my body and crawling across the floor towards her, I never did it.

I never had sex with her. We never had sex together. Amazing. And it's way better.

We got to know each other without all that stuff. So we feel for each other, like human beings.

God! It feels good! Right! Good!

*Pause.*

I don't have to tell you, do I? Shouldn't you have the fucking guts to tell me?

I have zero clue what you're talking about.

Did you ever change her diapers, Gary?

Oh my God, did you actually change her diapers?

What are you talking about, Peg?

I mean, that was kind of a joke, but it's entirely possible that you did.

What's going on here, Peg?

I got a call from Connie and Doug, Gary.

OK.

With the inground pool.

OK.

And the BBQs.

Yeah.

We went skiing with them.

I know.

Twice.

And?

To inform me you're being accused of assaulting their fifteen-year-old daughter.

*Pause.*

Sixteen.

Their daughter. They say you assaulted their daughter.

Impossible.

Physically impossible?

She missed the bus.

You drove her home?

There was a snowstorm.

It's April, Gary.

It was unsafe to continue.

She got home three hours late.

I was doing her a favour. We stopped by the side of the road and waited it out.

That's not what they're
saying.

They're saying you did a
dirty thing.

They're saying you did
several dirty things.

They're saying you dirtied
their little girl.

Me?
What do you want to tell
me?


We're the same age, Gary.


They're saying you stalked
her,


On the internet—

and at school—

and outside of school.

That you followed her
around.

That you leered at her,

And you groped her,

Nothing dirty happened.


Connie and Doug.


Jesus. Let me tell you
something about


Connie and Doug.


And you, actually.



This is the problem.
You guys… all you guys are
just so…fuckin' *old*.

In years.
It never happened.


How could I have stalked
her?

She was…

She was my star player.

I didn't have to stalk her.


I was with her every day.

We were friends.

We worked together.

and tricked her.

I coached her.
And we won!
We won! We won the OFSAA
championship!
I have the medal to prove it!
We worked hard together.
And we won!
What did you ever win, Peg?
She missed the bus. I drove
her home.
We were waylaid by the
storm and—

And?

Nothing happened.
But even if it did.
This is. This is a long time
coming, Peg.

That is so beside the fucking
point, Gary.

It's not beside the fucking
point, Peggy.
It is not.
It is not beside the point.
It actually is the point.
They don't know what
happened.
What is happening actually,
between us.
And you don't either.

So what are you planning
here?
You going to wait for her to
graduate high school
and then come and live in
your basement apartment?

That's actually sort of the
plan, yes.

Does she know about this?

                She does, yes.

Sounds like she's had a
change of heart.

                She didn't bring the charges,
                Peggy, Connie and Doug
                brought the charges.

And how did they hear
about it? Talking drums?
Smoke signals?

                Nothing dirty happened.

Is that what you're going to
tell your union lawyer?

                I'm going to tell the truth.
                I'm going to say what the
                truth is.

Why in fuck would you do
that?

                Because I have nothing to be
                ashamed of, Peggy.
                Because this is hysterical.
                This is people, crazy.

Is that how she's come to
believe that you tried to
assault her in a car at the side
of the road?

                That just shows you, Peg.
                What did her parents tell
                you? What did you hear?

All of the above, Gary.
They said you touched her,
you touched her in the car.
Other things. I was shocked,
Gary.
Connie was out of control.
Doug was—I've never heard
his voice like that.

                She would never have said
                anything to incriminate me.

Three hours alone in a car at
the side of the road, during a
blizzard, in April.
What happened, Gary?
You're a teacher in a public
school.
If they smell blood they'll
come for you.

They're teachers, Peg.
They always smell blood.
I did not coerce her, in any
way.
I would never dream of that.
That's not what I want.
Coercion, forcing—this is
not part of what's going
on here.
These feelings I have—that
we have, she and me—are
good feelings.
And when they're good
feelings, there's no bad.
There's no badness.
There's no victim.
It's all good.
Except for you. Maybe.
Because even then.
I wouldn't be happy if I
stayed, Peg.
I wouldn't be happy, you
wouldn't be happy, and the
kids wouldn't be happy.

You going to be happy
dropping soap for tweakers
in Millhaven?
Teachers don't do well in
prison, Gary.

I didn't do anything wrong.

*PEGGY slaps him twice.*

You need to wake up.
You can't come back from
this, Gary.

> I am awake.
> She's woken me up.
> She's brought me back to life.
> Besides, they don't have any
> proof.

> *Pause.*

> Because it didn't happen,
> Peg.

Can you trust this girl?

> *Pause.*

Are you in love with this
girl?

> *Pause.*

Can you trust this girl?

> These feelings are not my
> fault, Peggy.
> They're not my fault.

She told, Gary.
She told.
And now you are going to
tell me.
You are going to tell me what
you should have told me
when all this began.

> How could I have told you?

By opening your mouth and
speaking the words, Gary.
By being a man.
I'm your wife.
Right?
Not that I really know what
that word means anymore.

But you didn't tell me, Gary.
And you didn't tell me not
because you were worried I
wouldn't understand.
You didn't tell me because
you were worried I *would*
understand.
Huddled together in the
snow with all your secrets.
Like you'd just caught a
tiger.
What did you do after, Gary?
Find the only store in Central
Ontario that still sells the
vinegar douche?
Forgive me for thinking the
worst about my husband,
but most people I know hate
pedophiles.
So now you're going to
tell me.
Now, when it's almost
too late.
Now you're going to open
up your mouth and say,
"aahh."

*Pause.*

Where do you think you'll
sleep tonight?
You think you might sleep
here tonight?

                              It's doubtful.

Good.

                              I'm gonna go. I got a free
                              night at the Super 8 with my
                              Domino's card.

Good. Get some sleep. Or
will you be too busy clearing
your hard drive.

You tell me.


So what happened in the
car?

Is that a euphemism?

If I harmed her, or any
underage girl, in any way,
then let me die in a hail of
gunfire.


She's brilliant, Peggy. You've
seen her play.
She's like a hunter with
that ball, like a bear with a
hedgehog.
I can't resist that
opportunity.
In fact, it's my job to do the
opposite, truth be told.
I wouldn't be doing my job if
I didn't take notice.

Isn't that right? Isn't it?

To farm and shape that
opportunity?
What if Tuck came to you?
With a sonnet or a play or
something.
And you read it. And it was
insightful.
You know, it said things.
You think you couldn't stop
yourself from making him
the best writer you could?
You don't have a
responsibility to make him
the best writer in the world?

I would. I do. But I wouldn't
fuck him.

You wouldn't have to.
He'd fuck you.
Aren't you women always
the victims?

Excuse me?

*Pause.*

You know what I mean
though, right?

Barely.

This is biological, Peggy.
She's…you know, she's at
the age where in another
time, in another place, she'd
be offered up for marriage
to like a local tribesman or
something.

What happened in the car,
Gary?

I did the best I could with
the situation at hand.

Did you touch her, Gary?

I did everything I could not
to touch her.

What happened in the car,
Gary?

And this was a good feeling.
A loving feeling.
And because I felt it for her I
was able to keep from doing
what I wanted to do.

Which was.

Cunnilingus mainly.
I wanted to perform
cunnilingus on her. For her.
With her.

Did you touch her, Gary?

It's impossible to never touch
someone, Peg.
So no. But yes.
Once.
On the volleyball court.
I placed my hand on the
small of her back and my
palm rested on her belly to
reposition her.

Twice:
My kneecaps brushed her
kneecaps when I took my
seat at the boys' basketball
championship—which we
lost 78-75.
I had turned to face
the back of the gym to
avoid—well—positioning
my derriere into the
students' faces. And as a
result my knees brushed
by her knees—kneecaps
and we—sort of as an
acknowledgment that it was
a disconcerting feeling to
have kneecaps touch in that
way—we looked into each
other's eyes.

Third time.
I pushed her hair out of her
eyes and I believe I very
slowly tucked it behind her
ear.
But that was out of
kindness and convenience
actually, because she was

concentrating on her Bunsen
burner and I was worried…
but perhaps that's irrelevant.
But aside from very gently
pushing her hair back
behind her ears. Or ear,
rather. Yes, ear, because at
that time she was wearing
her hair parted at the side
and it sort of swooped over
her face and I worried it
tickled her nose or not. That
time we did not look at
each other.
Our eyes did not meet at that
time. But I felt her attention,
because she was very still.
While she let me do it.

Did she touch you?

Yes, she did.
She spat—no, OK—that
wasn't quite a touch but
there was an exchange or
rather an exchange of bodily
fluids when she spat her
chewing gum into my hands
and her saliva touched
my—um—palm.
That wasn't an official touch
but it did warm my palm
and wet it.
And her saliva mixed with
my palm sweat while her
eyes looked into mine as
she…spat it out into my
hand while she looked at me.
So it was everything but
a touch there, but it was
quite…provocative.

I have to drink something.

Varsol? Windex? Molten
lead?

And that's it. Those four
times. That's it.

What can I get you?

*Pause.*

We didn't do anything
wrong.

What was she doing in our
car?

We'd missed the bus. She'd
missed the bus.
So I drove her home.
And there was a
blizzard — as you
know — and we waited by
the side of the road for about
two hours and forty-five
minutes.
There was no cell reception,
so we just waited it out.
And talked. We spoke.
That's it.

What did you talk about?

It was a private conversation.
I don't feel like I should
tell you every facet of
our communication that
afternoon.

What words were spoken?

It was the words that weren't
spoken, Peggy.

When did it start?

Where does a river begin?

I tried to look away, Peggy.
I promise.

I did my best.
It was inappropriate.
I knew that.
But every time I looked
at her.
She looked back.
Every time.
I'm not crazy to think that.

She loved you just like a
grown-up would.

This was a mature feeling
she had.

Isn't that cute?
Isn't that irresistible?

*PEGGY takes off her bathrobe. Underneath she is dressed in
a very short Catholic schoolgirl outfit.*

Gary.
I know you dream about a
different life.

I don't dream about it, Peg.
I'm living it.

Smell me. Here.

*She points to her midriff. He smells…*

Nothing?

Nope.

How about here?

*She pulls open her shirt and a breast flops out.*

Nope.

*She spreads her legs and guides his face down to her vagina.*

How about here. You smell
any of the mall puke in here?

Nope.

Give it a taste. See if you can
taste it.

What are you going to say,
no?

Peggy.

Gary.
Lick your wife's vagina.

*Pause.*

Notice anything different?

Yes.

I removed every single piece
of undesirable hair on my
body with a bottle of expired
Neet from the back of the
kids' cupboard. Starting
from ground zero.
And working out. My
labia. My clitoral hood. My
pudenda.
My thighs. My buttocks. My
knees. My shins. My belly.
My feet. My breasts. Put my
nipples in your mouth, Gary.

Wow.

Smooth as a baby's bottom.

Yeah.

And you want me now,
don't you?

Yeah.

So do it.

*She straddles him.*

I know it's not our regular
night, but damn the
torpedoes.
Fuck me on not our regular
night.

OK.

You wanna fuck me?

Yes.

You wanna fuck me because
I don't have any hair on
my body?

Yes.

Just like a little girl?

Peggy.

Just like a real little girl?

Pegs.

Did you touch her, Gary?
Like you're touching me.

No, Peggy. No no.

Fuck me like you fuck her,
Gary.

No, Peggy. You got the
wrong idea.

Fuck me, Gary. Fuck me.

Peggy.

*GARY comes.*

Jesus.

There are three reasons why
you should take the advice
I'm about to give you.
One. If you don't, I'll snip
your dick off with my angry
bald vagina and bury it in
the backyard for the dogs to
dig up.

Two and Three. Jaime and
Jessica.

After the sit-down,
deposition, trial, discipline
process is over—in fact,
exactly ten months from
now—arbitrarily, how
nice, Valentine's Day—you
will have an affair with a

co-worker: man, woman,
dog, insect, I give not a shit,
but he/she/it needs to be
over forty, divorced and/
or widowed and it needs to
ruin you.
You will ask me for
forgiveness, in front of your
daughters, on your hands
and knees, and I will politely
kick you out of the house
and we will begin friendly
separation proceedings.
Jaime and Jessica will not be
known as the daughters of a
pedophile.

                              *Pause.*


When you go to see your
union lawyer, garrotte this
little bitch.
But facts.
Nobody wants to know what
a forty-five-year-old man
feels at two in the afternoon
on a weekday.
It's embarrassing and
shameful.
With time, place, and
witnesses — convince
them that you distanced
yourself from this insane
nymphomaniac until
she coerced you — by
deliberately missing the
bus — to drive her home
from the tournament. And
then — alone at the side
of the road during a freak

snowstorm (how romantic)
she came on to you in
the confines of the car at
the side of a snowy road.
You heroically resisted
her charms and threats
and as a result she took
her revenge by somehow
convincing her parents
Connie and Doug, our old
friends—as outlandish as it
seems!—that her pathetic,
sex-starved, forty-five-year-
old volleyball coach, in the
throes of a mid-life crisis
and trying desperately to
relive his youth, to relive
his entire life, in fact,
attempted an unsuccessful
rape which—though it
left no physical scars or
evidence—will make her an
emotional wreck for years
to come.
A bitch, in fact. A classic
bitch.

On behalf of women
everywhere: thanks for being
a dick.
As per hominidae.
You need that translated,
Gary?
Like every other knuckle-
dragging cock-swinging
naked ape on Earth?

                    *Breath.*

Be that as it may:

*Breath.*

Does that sound like
something you might be
able to play out? Something
as outrageous as that? To
save your daughters from a
lifetime of humiliation?

                      I'll tell the truth.
                      I didn't do anything wrong.
                      I'm innocent.

Good, Gary. I almost
believed you there.
Lose some of the frail-little-
bitch from the eyes and
you'll have this.

                      Cupid's arrow, Peggy.

*Pause.*

You should have fucked
her, Gary.
You should have emptied
your balls into her.
Then at least you'd have
had the guts to shut up
about it.
Nothing shames a man
more than getting what he
wants.

## ACT TWO

*Two weeks later. A meeting room. BARBARA observes GARY for a time. Finally, she speaks.*

BARBARA:                          GARY:

Did you find the place all
right?

                                        I did, thanks, yeah.

Did you take the toll route?

                                        No.

Austerity measures?

                                        Something like that.

How are things at home?

                                        I don't see how that's any of
                                        your business.

*Pause.*

Do we have anything to
worry about, Gary?

                                        Nope.

*BARBARA points to a pile of Mercedes's printed testimony.*

That's quite a stack, isn't it?
She could have said anything
in there, Gary.
And did, in fact.
Seven hours of testimony.
So, let me suggest
something.

You're worried—or should
be—that you might have
something to worry about.
Because what's being
discussed here makes it
tough for anyone to come
out smelling like Teen Spirit.

OK.

I didn't want to come here
today.
I don't like you, or what you
didn't do.
But this came down from
Dave Wichert.
Who is, as you know, my
superior.
Three OFSAA championships
count for something, I guess.

Pride of a game well played,
mostly.

Sure.
If Middleton the "bra
burner"—yes, that's
how they refer to me,
these surprisingly
non-octogenarian white
men—will back him, we'll
pull an OJ.
And the school's reputation
will remain as unblemished
as the tawn of its youth.

Someone's on your side.
Is what I'm saying.

No need.
I plan to tell the truth.

Let's start there.
Tell me about Mercedes.

Mercedes is a wonderful
human being.

An excellent student.
And an amazing athlete.

That must have been
exciting.
To have a hand in a young
girl's development like that.
To be guiding her step
by step through physical
processes that are new and
wondrous to her.

It's the reason I became a
teacher.
The reason I became a coach.

I'm sorry your relationship
changed.

It didn't.

Mr. Adams.

She didn't bring the charges.

Who did?

Connie and Doug.

Their name is on it. But how
do you think they found
out?

Beats me.

Fear.

Innuendo.

Shame.

Shame. Definitely. Shame.

Sometimes it's hard to
distinguish what's right and
what's wrong.
Especially when it all feels so
darn good.

*Pause.*

That's why rules are helpful.

I'm glad to hear that, Gary.
Because grey areas tend to
smear.

Everybody gets a little on
them.

          There are no grey areas.

Are there not?

          Only details.

That might work.

    *BARBARA picks up a paper and consults it.*

A) Gary Adams willfully
encouraged the victim to
spend time alone with him—

          There's no victim.

There is a victim.
We just have to determine
who it is.
—willfully encouraged the
victim to spend time alone
with him outside of school
hours.

Cast your mind back, Mr.
Adams. Was there any time
you encouraged Mercedes
McPfefferidge to be alone
with you outside of school
hours.

          Encouraged?
          No.

Please. Take some time to
think about it.

         *Pause.*

Let the events of the last year
or so play out in your mind.

          Aside from the car?

The car is taken for granted.
The car is tsk, tsk, tsk…taken
for granted.

You coached her privately.

I did nothing outside the
conventional boundary of
teacher/student relationship.

On school property.
The union was fine with that.
As were Connie and Doug.

And these private coaching
sessions were always
chaperoned.

Chaperoned by…

Supervised.

Supervised. By John Phillips,
my assistant, or Claude
L'Atelier—a member of the
custodial staff.
There was always a third
party present. Supervising.
As per the union guidelines.

This chaperone—John
Phillips or Claude
L'Atelier—was there to be
sure that nothing unseemly
happened between you two.

Again, I hesitate to use the
word chaperone.

It's just a word, Gary.

But it suggests something
that is absolutely not true.

And what is absolutely not
true?

The need for a chaperone.
Supervisor is better.
I needed to protect myself.

Protect yourself from what?

In what way?

From being misunderstood.

In a way that would suggest I was in any way doing anything that would make the presence of a chaperone—

Supervisor.

No, a chaperone, necessary.

Because you weren't.

Because I wasn't.

Bravo, Mr. Adams.

That is her word, by the way.

Chaperone?

Yes.

Huh.

Surprised.

A little.

Flattered.

My feelings are irrelevant.

No. They're not.

*A moment. GARY bristles.*

What is your job exactly?

To get you off.

Like a two-dollar hooker.

You must be used to prices in Thailand.

*Another moment.*

What do you stand for, Barbara?

Do you want to call another lawyer?
Do you want to call a lawyer who stands for something?

Do I have a choice?

*A moment.*
*Then BARBARA calls GARY on his studied cockiness.*

Let me axe you a
hypothetical.

Shoot.

Thank you, Gary, I will.

Good, Mrs. Middleton.

Barbara.

(*A dig.*) Ms.?

Don't you think Mercedes
would have become a
better volleyball player if
you had been able to coach
her—without supervision?

*Pause.*

That's something you've
thought about.

It can be difficult to give
certain answers, or to
prescribe certain exercises,
when there is always
something reminding you
that what you're doing has
the potentiality to explode
into criminal behaviour.

Because what you felt made
you uneasy.

I didn't feel uneasy.

She mentions you were
uneasy.

She doesn't. I wasn't.

She mentions your
perspiration level.

She what?

She mentions that your
perspiration level increased.

We were working.

She was working.
You were coaching.

Which is—in a
gym—inevitably a workout.

So your perspiration level
had nothing to do with what
you were feeling.

Warm?

Could you demonstrate
what coaching looks like?

What do you mean, here?

Yes, just do a little coaching
in front of me here.

Now?

Yes, please. Do some
coaching here.

OK.

*GARY stands, does some things with his hands. Says some*
*coaching stuff.*

Thank you. Water?

No thanks.

Cigarette?

—

Because what you felt was
perfectly normal?
Because what you felt was
perfectly non-criminal?

What I felt was perfectly
none of your business.

That's fine, Mr. Adams.

That's not what we're here to
discuss, is it?

Personally? I don't even
want to know.
But professionally—it may
become important to define
exactly what your feelings
were for this girl.

*Pause.*

Is there not?

That's fine. It was tense.
You were tense, and sweaty
from—coaching.

What was?

I'm sure it was.
But next time, coach a little
harder if, you know, they ask
you to.

No, Mr. Adams. We may be
here for some time.
We can order vindaloo, if it
comes to it.

She says—said—that you
spent…
Seven minutes with her
alone after practice waiting
for her mother to pick her up
in the parking lot outside the
main entrance to the school.

And she reports that you
stood a few feet away
from her.
Two-and-a-half feet to be
exact.

There's no crime in feelings.

Of course there's no crime in
feelings.

It was an innocent comment.

The perspiration level
comment.

Is that all?

What else does she say?

I was doing my duty to
protect her.
She was a minor.
She was a fifteen-year-old
girl.

A permissible distance.

The sun was just going down
and you and she watched
a rabbit come out of its
hole and lope around the
boulevard leisurely eating
midwinter grass.
And she said that you
pointed out the way the
rabbit's fur glinted like gold
in the early evening sun.
And then she commented
that she felt like that rabbit
coming out of its hole when
she finished practice with
you. When she was "tired,
and glowing, and finding
something from nothing."
Her words.
But then you turned and
looked into her eyes.
As if to—and these are her
words—"confirm what she
had seen in herself."

Her words?

Yes.

I couldn't have said it better
myself.

If it comes to that, try.

Is it illegal to look into
someone's eyes?

Not yet.

And when she was asked
how long you stood a few
feet away from her she said
seven minutes—though she
admitted to some difficulty
in judging because time

seemed—as she said—to
"warp and flex when he
(you) was (were) around."

And you may ask how she
knew it was seven minutes
if indeed time was warping
because of these adolescent
stirrings for her capable
volleyball coach, but I'll
make a preemptive strike
here and tell you that it is
because she saw the clock on
the wall leaving the school,
and then saw the clock on
the dash of her mother's car
when she got into it.
Seven minutes.
Or thereabouts.
That's the thing with girls in
love, I guess.
Every detail is memorable
and important.
It's like they're living in a
novel.

    I'm a Phys Ed teacher.

Did that happen?

    You tell me.

Do you have a drinking
problem?

    What else does she say in
    there?

In the fullness of time, Mr.
Adams.
Just answer honestly.
Did that happen?
That you stayed in the
same spot.
Exactly two-and-a-half feet
from her.

Staring—sorry,
looking—sorry, having eye
contact with a beautiful
volleyball champion for
seven minutes in which you
point out poetic aspects of a
winter scene.

That's a long time to look at
somebody.
A lot happens in that time.

> *A long pause while they look at each other—like a staring
> contest. BARBARA is the first to claim victory.*

See?

I mean, that's reportage.
That's not—intent.
So…

It's details, Gary.
And it's flirting.
It's called encouraging her to
spend time alone with you.

How?

I like that you wear your
näiveté like a shield,
Mr. Adams.

B) Gary Adams discussed
matters of a sexual nature
with the victim.

How did you obtain
Mercedes McPfefferidge's
e-mail address?

From her father, Doug.

What did Doug say? "Why
don't you start e-mailing
my teenaged daughter
privately?"

Of course not.

You're aware that e-mail
correspondence between
teacher and student requires
a chaperone as well.

Supervision?
I cc'd her father. I cc'd Doug
on every one.

Every time?

Good for you.

Habit.

Thank you.

One said her serve was
"catlike."

You've seen her play,
Barbara.

It said—quote—"It's like
a wild animal has stepped
into my gym. I have to force
myself to stop watching you
to help the other players."
End quote.

I cc'd Doug on that one.
As a proud father myself, I
didn't think he'd mind.

High praise.

I'm not going to deny that I
was taken with Mercedes's
volleyball playing.
I don't think I should
have to.
You only get a player like
that coming along once
every, I don't know, you
know?
And this is my profession.
I assume—assumed—Doug
understood that.
Maybe the words I used
were a bit flowery but my
motives were clean.

Situation being what it was.
It's all you can do.

Situation being what what
was?

Situation being what
was—you know—I had a
tremendous athlete on my
hands here.
And my enthusiasm needed
to be checked here and there,
sure, who doesn't love their
work, because…you know…
she was really good.

Good for you.

And the team. And her
future. She had a great
future.

Surely she still does.

What.

Have a great future.
Even without you.
She's still playing, Gary.

Except I'm not coaching her
now.

No.
Someone else is coaching her
now.

Who is coaching her now?

*BARBARA watches GARY.*

Is that a concern of yours?

I invested in that girl.

You did.
And now someone else is
investing in that girl.

*Little pause.*

It doesn't matter.

But like you said.

He'll never do what I could
do.


It'll be a battle for her not to
lose.

We're not here to discuss
your feelings.

Exactly.

I'm not your therapist.


How close are you to Doug?

Close. Not as close as we
were.


Close enough to know
that he changed his e-mail
address two years ago?

Was I aware of that?

Were you?

I was not. Was I?

Were you?

I don't think so. Was I?

Phew, Mr. Adams!
Because the problem here
is…
Well, it's the content.

*She reads.*

Quote: "You are a visit from
Mount Olympus.
I can't take my eyes off of
you. Your soul seems to
guide you like an angel, at
times avenging, at times
forgiving, but with a single
purpose: to win, but more
than that, to grace us mere
mortals with the presence
of a champ. If it were
appropriate, I would drop
to my knees in worship.

And stay there until asked
to rise again. But it is
'inappropriate' — to use the
language of this workaday
world — like so many other
things you deserve. From
me to you, encouragement,
devotion, and commitment."
End quote.

> I cc'd her dad on that one. I
> cc'd Dougie on that very one.

*Pause.*

You've coached her since
when?

> Three years.

Since she was thirteen.

*Pause.*

> Fourteen.

*Pause.*

There is no crime in feelings,
Mr. Adams, but even you
can see that we have a little
crime going on here, can't
you?

> The crime of what, exactly?

Among others. Among
many others — quote — it is
"inappropriate like so many
other things you deserve
from me." End quote.

> That's not what I said.
> Typed.

I think it is, Mr. Adams. But
more importantly, they'll
think it is.

> That's not how it reads.

There's a period between deserve and from.
"...like so many other things you deserve, period, from me to you—colon — encouragement, devotion etc."

A period.

A period. A little dot. That stops things from being connected.

Which is exactly why you put it in there.

Barbara. You're reaching.

They have so much evidence, Mr. Adams.
Details and details and details.
This investigation rivalled the parsing of Monica Lewinsky's underwear drawer.

And you turned up this?

Among many other things.

Congratulations, Barbara. I believe this is the easiest case you've ever had to defend.

*Pause.*

How old was she when you drove her home from the tournament?

Sixteen.

Fifteen?

Sixteen.

On the day you drove her home from the tournament.

Sixteen.

How do you know that?

What date in April?

Because her birthday—as
the whole school knows this,
by the way—is in April.

The twenty-seventh. Two
weeks ago.

How does the whole school
know that?

Did you exchange gifts with
her on her birthday?

It's very difficult not to
notice these things.

GARY *blinks, thrown off for a moment.*

It seems it might be natural.
A good luck charm, or a
small package...

Does it say that in there?

Is that what she says in
there?

*Pause.*

And you knew it was her
birthday, that she had turned
sixteen, how exactly?

Because of the morning
announcements.
Because of the decorated
locker her friends made her.
Because this is Mercedes
McPfefferidge.

On Friday you saw these
things.
And heard them.

Does it say that about the
charm in there?

Because the difficulty here
is: any token from teacher to
student has an open-ended
interpretation attached to it.
Know what I mean?

Enlighten me.

Well. If you were to have
given her a gift. A gold
volleyball. Small. Classy.
At the end of a thin, gold
chain, for example.

*GARY laughs, with some rue, some astonishment.*

In, on, or around her
birthday, it would suggest,
to much dirtier minds
than either yours or mine,
that you were intent on
romancing the child, or
seducing her.

She's not a child.

Because?

She was sixteen.

So did you give her
anything?

What does she say in there?

I'm your lawyer, not hers.

So what does she say in
there.

*A moment.*

She says you are completely
innocent of giving her a
package, containing a gold
volleyball charm, that was
small, classy, and attached to
a thin gold chain.

*A small wave of relief passes over GARY's face. He shrugs.*

Then I guess I never did.

Which—according to her
teammates—she wore to
her championship game on
Sunday, the twenty-ninth,
hours before you drove
her home.

She couldn't have worn it if I
never gave it to her.

And the word of nine other
fifteen- or sixteen-year-old
girls would mean nothing
at all.
They all saw it, Mr. Adams.
Hidden in plain sight doesn't
work, especially in a girls'
locker room.
See, here's the problem:
intent.
A disciplinary committee
will see that locket as proof
of intent.

Intent of what, wishing my
star player luck?

Intent of seduction, or of
romance.
Both of which are illegal
before a girl's sixteenth
birthday.
But something tells me you
brushed over your tracks on
that one.
Or tried to.

Because the one we're most
concerned with here.

Sure.

is the third one.
C) "Gary Adams did invite
the victim to touch or caress
parts of his body with parts
of her body."

And.

She said you held hands
with her.

*Pause.*

And?

She says that you held her
hand.

What?

She says you held hands.

I held hands.

Was that a question?

What exactly did she say?

That you held her hand. You
held hands.
Specifically, in the car
coming back from the
OFSAA tournament in Sault
Ste. Marie.

That's the charge?

That's the charge.

That's. Excuse me. But that's
retarded.

Is it.

Isn't it?

In what sense retarded?

In the sense that…well…I
was expecting the charge
to be about something…
different than that.

Were you.

Well. Yes.
Weren't you?
Something…different.
Something outlandish.

Disappointed?

*GARY chuckles lightly.*

No.

Is it true?

—

Did you hold her hand?
Did you ask her to hold
hands?

Specifically, in the car.
On the way back from the
Sault.

*Looking at BARBARA, GARY smirks.*

          There's nothing else?

—

          In your intimidating stack?

*GARY watches BARBARA.*

          What a wonderful girl.

That's refreshing candour.

          Kids these days.

I'm not sure what you mean.

          Don't you? Barbara?
          Hear that silence?
          That's the sound of your
          bluff being called.

Excuse me?

          Laugh for once in your life;
          it's over.

You confident of that?

          110%. There's no volleyball
          charm.
          Nowhere.
          I guarantee it.
          And that's what it hangs on.
          No matter what you
          dredge up, or however
          you and Connie and Doug,
          and Peggy and John and
          the rest of you assholes
          interpret what she may
          have said or may not have
          said—we're pure.
          We're the love you dreamed
          about.

          If the glove don't fit, you
          must acquit.

This sounds like the reckless
hope of a young lover,
Mr. Adams.
Surely you don't still plan to
see her?

It would be unwise for me to
disclose that.
But just because I like you,
Barb.
And because you're cute
when you try so hard.
If and when it happens:
her pussy's going to be like
peaches and cream.
Soft, sticky, wet, and forever
fresh.

I'm learning a lot here.

And she'll have it till I'm
dead.
It's tough for you chicks,
I know.
But the sooner you accept
that, the sooner you can
begin to make your own
wise choices.

*Pause.*

But did you hold her hand,
Gary?
Like a teenager, Gary?
Because, I'll be honest, if
you did, it's going to be
hard to assert there wasn't a
little back-and-forth on this
relationship here.
A little I-scratch-your-back-
you-scratch-mine.
With a fifteen-year-old girl.

Whom you'd been coaching
since she was thirteen.

Barbara.
I've done nothing
wrong. And—more
importantly—I've done
nothing to be ashamed of.
Seven hours of conjecture
or no.
I didn't fuck her, Barb.
I didn't do anything illegal.

This is where you fail to
understand, Gary.
You should have got her
birthday right.

I did get her birthday right.

Because of the morning
announcements, on a Friday.
Because of her decorated
locker, on a Friday.
Because this was Mercedes
McPfefferidge, on a Friday.

Yes.

It's called a send-off, Gary.
It was her birthday weekend,
yes.
But her actual birthday.
Her sweet sixteen.
Was on the Monday.
The day after you returned
from the Sault.

The day after the snowstorm
whose freak arrival may or
may not have charmed the
pants off of either one of you.

Two days after you didn't
give her the charm.
She turned sixteen.

That arbitrary number that
means so much to all decent
citizens everywhere.
That could really raise the
temperature on this student/
teacher relationship.
This relationship that will
make members of the board,
the PTA, and the federal
police very uncomfortable.

                              Nothing dirty happened.

You're basically being
charged with pedophilia,
Gary.
Underage and under your
guardianship.
So nothing dirty had to
happen.
The charges are enough.
If she was fifteen, or even
near fifteen, you're in
trouble.
Nobody trusts anyone who's
maybe done what you've
maybe done.
Why should they?
It's the easiest decision a
parent could make.

                    *Pause.*

Do I detect a quail?

                              See, here's the thing. Here's
                              where I wonder who had a
                              hand in what where.
                              Because if Dougie found out
                              that I had used an old e-mail
                              address to cc him—which
                              I didn't do—at least not

knowingly—seriously—
then he might have kind of
trumped things up a bit here.
And if there's some talk
about this charm that
never got given, I think
Dougie and Connie
probably—like when
they finally understood
that I didn't actually do
anything wrong—like,
physically wrong with their
daughter—nothing evil,
nothing like a monster,
you know—they probably
wanted to get things going
a bit.

There we go, Mr. Adams.
A little sip of the Kool-Aid.

If there was some way that
we could maybe sit in the
same room. If we could all
get together and just hash
this out.

It's too late for that.

If there was a way to get
Dougie and Mercedes and
Connie and Peggy and you
and me—

It's not going to happen.

Together in the same room,
we could just hash this out.

It's not going to happen.

But why? Why? How is
this serving anyone's best
interest?
To stop communication.

Mr. Adams.

To stop people from talking
to each other. People need to
see how Mercedes and I are
together.
There's nothing wrong here.

Keep it together. You're
not doing yourself—or
me—any favours here.

I'm sorry.
I'm frustrated.

I can see that.

This is so much more
complicated than
this—procedure can
uncover.

I'm sympathetic.
In fact, that's my job, believe
it or not.

There are grey areas.

Details.
I'm part of the union too,
believe it or not.

Jesus.

We're both pursuing the
same thing here.
Try to look beyond my balls-
busted-at-bat average and
remember: if you've actually
done nothing wrong, now's
your chance. Now's your
opportunity.
Defend yourself.
Come clean.
Provide me with some
context.

*Pause.*

Things being what
they are—seven hours
of testimony from a
fifteen—(*Preempting GARY's
protest.*) sorry, *fifteen*-year-old
girl—against a forty-five-
year-old teacher—things
are tilting out of your favour
right now. And that's not me
talking.
That's the testimony talking.
That's the stuff we'll have to
face in court together.
I'm part of the union too.
And I have something to
gain from this.
Can we help each other out?
Can you give me a little
context?

If you've done nothing
wrong, have your day.
It's your right. As a
citizen—in fact, as a
wronged citizen, it's your
duty.
Fight this foolish girl. Fight
this girl.
Fight her family.
Make it so they don't do this
again to any other teacher
who takes an interest in her
best interests.

She's already sold you out,
Gary.
Her parents wouldn't have
brought the charges if she
hadn't already sold you out.

                                    Have you ever been in love?

Oh yes. Very much so.

How old do you think I am?

A middle-aged man is a wolf
in skin clothing.

Was I?

How old are you?

So you know.

You were married.

It's the tick of the clock.
Surely you can relate.

*In spite of how she feels, BARBARA chooses
to display sympathy.*

They should put something
in the staffroom coffee.

Saltpeter, inhalants, shingle
tar.
Anything to stop the
grinding, grinding, grinding.

Did she make promises she
didn't keep?

Has she contacted you since
the incident?

Can you trust her, Gary?

*A moment.*

I don't know.
I don't know.
Can I?

You're her first love.
But she is your last.

You want to throw your life
away to protect her?
What about you, Gary?
Who's going to protect you?

At the beginning of this
interview, I asked whether
you had supervisors at your
private volleyball sessions.

And you said yes, because
you needed to protect
yourself.
Protect yourself from what,
Gary?

Protect myself from people
like you.

I don't think that's true,
Gary.
I think you needed to protect
yourself from her.
Didn't you?
Just a little bit?

Even from her purity.
Because this report is
spotless.
These seven hours are
virginal.
Like, way more virginal than
anyone could believe.

I looked at her first. I think
I looked at her first. I'd try
to catch her unaware. Like
a deer in the forest. But she
would always look up at me.
She would always catch me.
Her eyelids would always
flutter open.
And in the beginning she
always smiled.
Because she was young
and unaware. And then
in the middle she didn't
smile, because something
was happening, and it was
dangerous.
And then in the end she
smiled again.

I knew everything about her.
How could I have got her
birthday wrong?

I won't say anything to
incriminate her.

I don't want to say anything
that's going to wreck her life.

Wishful thinking?


She was fifteen. She's not
going to jail, Gary.


Of course not.
I'm not asking you to lie,
Gary.
That's called perjury.
And no offence, but my
career means far more to me
than you do.
I'm just asking for context.
All alone with you.
In your car.
During a freak blizzard.
Trapped at the side of a
snowbound highway.
When you were driving
her home from a volleyball
tournament.
Couldn't you just remember
something that might help
us here?
About the hand-holding?
About who grabbed whose
hand first?
Give me a fact or two, Gary.

It was a pure moment.

I'm sure it was, sweetie.
But just think about what she
was feeling.
And what you were feeling.
And maybe there was a little
tug one way or the other.

Imagined or otherwise?
Is that something you can
remember?
A little tug?
One way. Or the other.

This is it, Gary.
This is pretty much the one.
This is pretty much the grey
area.
The only one.
Right here.
So.
What happened.

Just say it, Gary.

*GARY hesitates.*

She took my hand.
As I remember.

Who took whose hand?

She reached over and took
my hand.

Did she direct it toward her
breast or lower midsection?

I think so, yes.

Breast or lower midsection?

Both?

Which one first?

Breast?

Next.

Lower midsection.

And what did you do?

I ... pulled it away.

Good for you.
And how much time had
passed?

I'm not sure.

It's better to be sure, Gary.

Was there a clock on the
dash?

                Nope.

          *BARBARA sighs.*

Was there a song playing on
the radio?

                Yes.

What was it?

                "Shut Up and Dance with
                Me," by Walk the Moon.

Chorus or verse? (*A little
impatient now.*)
Teachers don't do well in
prison, Mr. Adams.

                Chorus.

Full?

                Half.

If pressed could you sing it?

                I'll sing.

Good boy.

## ACT THREE

*A Quality Inn-type hotel room. MERCEDES, dressed in her volleyball uniform, sits waiting, her full backpack beside her. A little pause. Then singing comes from behind the room door. It opens.*

MERCEDES:

Mr. Adams?

Mr. Adams.

I'm not—

I'm not supposed to talk to you.

And you're not supposed to talk to me.

GARY:

Happy birthday to you,

Happy birthday to you.

Happy Birthday, Mercedes McPfefferidge…

Happy birthday to you.

Don't. It's best that you don't.

We could just stand here then.
And look at each other.

*They do. And then—feeling silly—they smile a little, in spite of everything.*

You used to sing better.
What are you doing here?

Witnessing an undeserved defeat, of course.

Mr. Adams.
The bus will be here any
minute.
And it's not entirely
appropriate that you're here.

It's not entirely appropriate.
It's entirely inappropriate, in
fact.

I'm not supposed to see you.

According to the
stipulations.
Good for you.
See?
Maybe I passed something
useful along.

You think?

I pray daily.

Does it help?

It's just the last little bit of
my brain too chicken to kill
itself.

Don't you think the
stipulations protect you as
much as they protect me?

*GARY changes the subject.*

Slice?

No, Mr. Adams.

John Phillips sucks.

You were better?

Just think about that for
a moment and then give
yourself the answer.

We deserved to lose.

You never deserve to lose.
You just weren't as good
today as you once were.

I was farting sideways.

*Pause. Then they both laugh.*

I think when Claude L'Atelier said that in French it had more class.

It just sounded like it did because you're small-minded.

No. The French just get to do more with less judgement.

You coaching? At your new school?

How are the girls?

Boys. No good.

They hate me. They never visit. What else is new?

No, the team.

Not allowed. Part of the stipulations.

You were good, Mr. Adams.

The dream continues.
You're sure you don't want a slice of this?
I baked it myself.

(Smiling.) Gross.
I have to go.

MERCEDES begins to leave.

You've been losing a lot.

How do you know?

Internet. Your games are on the internet.

This picture you're painting of yourself is very sad.

It's the only way I can keep up.
St. Catharines. It's an island of shit.

Distracting yourself with any of your more promising players?

Boys can't play volleyball.
No finesse.
No strategy. No teamwork.

Girls are best.

Girls are best.

You changed your
deodorant.

*Pause.*

Mr. Adams. I feel like this
is the moment I walk out
of here.

I'm sorry. I'm sorry.

*MERCEDES pulls out her phone.*

This is Randy. He's my
boyfriend.

What a chump.

He's very kind.

Don't lose at this, too.

Ha ha, Mr. Adams. You're
the last person who should
talk to me about losing.

*GARY grabs the phone from MERCEDES —*
*as if playing keepaway.*

Seriously. Look at the — what
is that — what is happening
there — is that frosting in his
hair? Are you dating a man
with frosted tips?

Randy is a brilliant
swimmer.

Gay.

*(Torturing him.)* He's not gay.

*Pause.*

Here's my girl. Jaime.
This picture is old.
I get a new one at Christmas.
One a year.

Peggy's mad at you, eh?

It's something more than
that.

It's something women feel
when men betray them.

Life is choices.

You should have done
counselling. My parents
loved it.
They did it for two years
before they got divorced.

*Pause.*

She's the same age in this
picture as when I met you.

So serious.

*GARY makes a face. Then he gets up and starts doing The
Running Man—or some other ridiculous dance.*

This is serious.

*They laugh. Laughter subsides.*

So how would you feel if Mr.
Phillips started dating your
daughter?

Dating?

Hooking up with.

Is that the word you use
now?

Dating. Taking her on
dates. Or hanging around
her like you used to hang
around me.

I'd strangle him until his
eyes fell like warm oysters
onto my trembling hands.

I controlled myself
around you.

I know you did, honey.

We did our best.

We did.

But you got in here, Mr.
Adams. *(Taps her head.)*
You got in there right from
the beginning.

How embarrassing.

False modesty is
unattractive.
There was nothing
embarrassing about it.
I loved that time.
Your attention made me
grow.

All I did was coach you.

And Mr. Phillips coaches
me now.

And you lost today.

Fuck you, Mr. Adams.

Fuck you, too.

Well, I'm glad we had this
little talk.

I'm always glad to talk to
you.

Mr. Adams, when you say it
like you mean it, I feel like
you mean it.

I do.
I did.
And I will.

I have to go, Mr. Adams.

*She starts to leave.*

Camel driving the bus?

*(Stopping.)* Jesus Christ, did
you call her that too?

It is her!? I was joking,
almost, I guess. But wow.
She must be a hundred years
old.

Maybe she's never been born
and she'll never die.

Stuck behind the wheel of
a school bus in Southern
Ontario. What did she do
in her former life to deserve
that fate?

She probably was an old
gym teacher who fucked a
student.

*Pause.*

Mercedes. We never had
sexual intercourse.

Are you telling me that?
What is happening here?
Are you informing me
of that?
Is this new information
for me?

It's important to keep in
mind.
It was my insurance policy.

That's why you won't
spend eternity like Camel,
snapping gum and
screaming at children.
But was it worth it?

So far, no.

You're better off. I've seen
you drive.

All hunched over the wheel
of your third-hand Kia
Sorrento.
You know you drive like a
little old lady, right?

> I'm what's known as a
> cautious driver.

I'll never be like that.
I'll drive it like I mean it.

> I was trying to keep up with
> the school bus.

That's something as a grown
man you should never
admit.

> For what reason?

Many. But mainly because
it's so fucking lame.
Bore out your cylinders,
soup it up, drive it like you
mean it.
YOLO, yo.

> (*What the*) fuck is with age?

Exactly.

*Pause.*

Mr. Adams.

> Yes, Miss McPfefferidge.

Give me a piece of my
birthday cake.

> You got time?

Yeah fuck it, I'll slam it in.

> That's what she said.

Inappropriate and
unappreciated.

*They low-five.*

> They were wrong. We can
> talk about sex. We can joke.
> Nothing's wrong.

*GARY serves her a slice of the cake.*
*He waits patiently for her reaction.*

Seriously? This cake is
delicious.

I baked it with love.

This could—with work and
dedication—be a second
career for you. And bakers
are all old and ugly, right? So
it would be, you know, un-
dangerous?

I have a poster of Farah
Fawcett Majors on my wall.
The same one I had as a kid.
My mum made me remove
my stuff from her storage
locker.
That's how sad it's become.
I eat Dr. Sub almost every
day.
I bite it, like I'm a locust, my
head tilts back and forth.
I jab my jaws out at the food
in my folded hands until I
puke a little.
That way I know I'm done.
I'm full.

You ruined me, Mercedes
McPfefferidge.
I'm on the shuttle to the
other side now.
It used to bother me to think
about retirement, and the
calendar I saw in my head,
flipping and flipping.
But now, since I taste nothing
but mustard and pepper, I
sort of can't wait.

I try to kick-start my
optimism in the morning,
but by lunch I'm staring at
the staffroom clock, counting
the minutes I've got left.
It's an astoundingly large
number.
Ten million-odd, five
hundred and twelve
thousand-odd.
Was it better when it all went
by too fast?

Finished?

All done.

Let me take that.

Thank you.

Thank you.

No. Thank you.

*(Sincere, meaning more.)*
No. Thank you.

*(Accepting what he offers.)*
Thank you.

You're welcome.

That wasn't so hard, was it?

That's what she said.

Seriously, Mr. Adams? Nice
apology. It means something.

No problem. When you're
sorry, you're sorry.

Not enough, but...I loved
you, Mr. Adams.

I love you too.

*Pause.*

If you don't leave for your
bus soon, I'm going to come
apart at my seams.

Mr. Adams.

I should go.

Call me Gary.

Wanna bump? Like our
phones? We could bump
them.

What is that?

I have an app. On my
phone. We bump our phones
and our information gets
transferred through the air
and ends up in each other's
phones.
We don't even have to touch.

I don't think I can do that,
Mr. Adams.

Seriously, it'll be fun. Let's
do it.

Umm. No.

*Pause. MERCEDES turns to go.*

So what went wrong today?

Amanda's and my timing
was off, and our back
defence was crap.

There was a subtlety that
you always had that wasn't
at work.

When you're right, you're
right, Mr. Adams.

Call me Gary.

All right, Mr. Adams.

That subtlety was
inspiration.
You didn't have any
inspiration.

I can't inspire you,
Mr. Adams.
Not anymore.

I have like, five minutes.

You shouldn't.
But you do.

Run away with me.

*Taken aback, she revives an old joke,*
*the one about the school dance.*

Wood Eye!

Harelip! Harelip!
Seriously. Move in with me
and fuck the odds.
Fuck John Phillips. Fuck this
school.
Fuck them all.

In a basement apartment in
St. Catharines?

We could work on your
college applications.
We'll work together at the
kitchen table.
And check the mail every
day until we get the offer we
want.
We could get you a
scholarship to an American
university.
A full scholarship to Brigham
Young.
Imagine that?
They have a campus on
Maui.
And I could coach you the
whole way.
You're too good for this
place.

I believed what you told me
in the car.
I believed what you said.

I did too.

I still do.
Next stop: the Olympics.
I meant it then. I mean it
now.
This is the moment.
Right now.
We can trust our bravery.
This is the moment that we'll
look back on when we see
ourselves on the Jumbotron,
waving to all the suckers
back home.
The ones too chicken to do
what we did.
Too chicken to take a big risk
on our big love.

And then what would your
parents think of me?

They'd still hate you,
Mr. Adams.
You got up in front of all
those people and said some
terrible things about me.

Your parents, pardon my
French, are fucking idiots.

Mr. Adams. My whole life is
like, in front of me.

So's mine.
They made it dirty, not us.
Cupid's arrow. Nothing to be
done.

We just held hands. I don't
remember how our hands
came together. They just did.

That's what you told them.

It was the truth. And it was
what made it true.

We barely spoke.

It wasn't supposed to snow
that day.
All the weather reports said
clear sailing.
And I noticed bluebells on
the highway going up.
How could it have snowed?
Everything was working in
our favour.

But that's not what you told
them.

*(He sings softly.)* "So don't
you dare look back, you keep
your eyes on me…"
We were so alone together in
that car.
With the snow piling up on
the windows.
Your eyes changed colour
with the light.
"this woman is my destiny…
you are my destiny…"

Was I alone in that car?

I felt it too, Mr. Adams.
Doesn't that count?

I was right to trust you.

And I was wrong to trust
you.

It was the most beautiful
moment of my life.
It was like lightning hitting
an old, dusty castle.

*GARY makes a thunder and lightning sound.*

I'm your Frankenstein.
I'm aliiiiiiiivvveee!
Doesn't that count?

I waited for a text, an e-mail.
And none came.


How did she find out?


I don't have access.
Ignorance is bliss.


For you to be on that side of
the room, and for me to be
on this.
Never coming together,
never coming apart. But
standing, looking, and
talking around the issue.
That would be basically close
to perfect.

My mother, Mr. Adams.
She took my phone,
cancelled my e-mail.

Parents don't like it when
old men sniff around their
teenage daughters.
You wouldn't.

What do you want, Mr.
Adams?

But Mr. Adams. One time we
had that.
And it was perfect.
But then you fucked it all up.
You did.
I don't know who you are,
Mr. Adams.

I'm sorry, Mercedes.

If it was true love, I could
have been any age.

Don't be naïve.

Because I wanted you to
fight for me?
Because I expected you to
feel like I did?
To fight for our love.

To stand up on a chair and
say, "I love this girl"?

I couldn't have done that.

But me, lying awake all
night, sweating through my
pyjamas over a man who has
hair in his ears is OK?

Why did you lie?

This is how the world works,
Mercedes.
I had no choice.

You could have protected
me.
You could have said what
happened.
We didn't do anything
wrong.

In your eyes.

In yours too, right?

Everything that feels good
feels guilty.

It's why I'm not in St.
Catharines with you.

I fucked up. I lied to save
myself.
I made it seem like you
did something which you
didn't do.
I did it to save myself.
But I did it to save you, too.

I wasn't able to open my
locker for two years
without used condoms
falling out of it.
People really didn't like me.
And I didn't win today.

You're going to win again.
But you have to be with me.

I don't know anymore,
Mr. Adams.

It's the price we had to pay.
Who cares what these people
think?
We're going to rise above all
of them.

I don't know.

They got me, too.

You got you.

Did I ruin you for all the
other boys?

Men, Mr. Adams.
Today I enter the arena of
grown men.
Isn't that why you're here?
Because I'm finally old
enough for you to work your
way into?
Well, take it all, bitch.

Mercedes.

I shouldn't have wasted my
first love on you.
You know it never comes
back.
That's why you came to me
in the first place.
Because you wanted
something you can never
have again.
And you used me to get it.
And you didn't deserve it.

You'll get over it.
You're young.

I'm over it right now,
dick-smack.
Truth hurts, Mr. Adams.

I deserve everything you say.
But I came today to bring
you this.

*GARY pulls out a small, elaborately wrapped gift.*

I'd prefer not, Mr. Adams.

*GARY holds out the present. At some point in the next speech*
*MERCEDES takes the present and starts to unwrap it.*

> When I woke up on my
> forty-fifth birthday, all the
> choices I ever made were
> stupid.
> And there was no going
> back.
> I was in a tunnel with
> no exits.
> Only forward, with weekly
> sex that was like shoving
> a semi-filled water balloon
> into a mail slot.
>
> And then you walked in.
> And you had it all before
> you.
> And I started to believe that
> I could reverse all those
> choices.
> If I got to know you, if I got
> to love you.
> If I got you to love me.
> My whole life could get
> corrected.
> And then I was done.

I've got three minutes,
Mr. Adams.

> For you.
> On your eighteenth.

*It is a gold volleyball charm on the end of a thin, gold chain.*

Oh wow.

The arrow came from
elsewhere.
The arrow came from outer
space.

You shouldn't have.

I should have.

You don't have this kind of
money.

I had to.

Mr. Adams, you teach
part-time.

In St. Catharines.

And you live in a basement
apartment.

Exactly.
You're the only thing that
means anything to me.

How did you know I threw
the old one out?

What else would you have
done?
You thought it would hang
on that.
But it didn't.
It hung on me, lying.
So let me make up for it.
Let me give you a new one.
Free of baggage. Free of
charges.

Good one, Mr. Adams.

Can I put it on you?

I don't know, Mr. Adams.
The bus is like, right outside.

It'll just take a second.
I've been practising for days.

*MERCEDES allows GARY to put the necklace on her.*

Mr. Adams.

Let's just sit tight for a while.

*GARY stands behind MERCEDES and fastens the clasp on the necklace.*

> Listen. Our hearts are
> beating in time.

*GARY is so intense he has bitten his lip. Blood trickles down from his mouth.*

Are you bleeding,
Mr. Adams?

> It's nothing.

*Taken aback, MERCEDES switches decisively.*

I think I did something
wrong.

> You couldn't have done
> anything wrong.
> You were fifteen.

I'm not going anywhere
with you.
I'm going to catch the bus
home.

*MERCEDES starts to leave. GARY stops her.*

> You shouldn't have been
> looking at me like you were
> looking at me.

(*Wheeling.*) How was I
looking at you!

> When a girl looks at a man
> like that, she gives him the
> guts to continue.

But you didn't have the guts
to continue, Mr. Adams.

> But I do now.
> Let's kill this thing.

What thing?

> Let me fuck you out of me.

*MERCEDES shoves GARY to the ground.*

Mr. Adams. Be a gentleman.

*GARY gets up and advances again.*

It's like poison, this shit.
Let me blow it into your
young body.
Let me blow all my oldness
into you.

*MERCEDES socks GARY right in the nose. GARY falls.*

Grow up, Mr. Adams.

*MERCEDES gathers her stuff and heads out.*

*GARY sits on the bed for a while.*
*Blood starts to drip from his nose.*

*After a time, he reaches over to the room telephone.*
*Presses "0." A pause.*

I want to change rooms.
I want to stay in this room.

*Pause.*

Gary Adams.

*Pause.*

You have that on file. Just
switch it to this room.

*Pause.*

Do I have to say?

*A little pause.*

Indefinitely.

*GARY hangs up. Sits.*

*A moment.*

*GARY grabs the rest of the cake. He eats it with his hands, at first slowly, then mashing it into his face, never able to get enough.*